SOUL H₂O

40 Thirst Quenching Devotions for Women

Be refreshed ♡ Sherry

Sherry Stahl

Founder and Author of the Soul H2O Blog

SOUL H2O
Copyright © 2016 by Sherry Stahl

Unless otherwise indicated, all Scripture taken from THE HOLY BIBLE, NEW INTERNATIONAL VERSION®, NIV® Copyright © 1973, 1978, 1984, 2011 by Biblica, Inc.® Used by permission. All rights reserved worldwide. Scripture quotations marked (NLT) are taken from the Holy Bible, New Living Translation, copyright © 1996, 2004, 2007 by Tyndale House Foundation. Used by permission of Tyndale House Publishers, Inc., Carol Stream, Illinois 60188. All rights reserved. Scripture taken from The Message. Copyright © 1993, 1994, 1995, 1996, 2000, 2001, 2002. Used by permission of NavPress Publishing Group. Scripture quotations marked (KJV) taken from the Holy Bible, King James Version, which is in the public domain. Scripture quotations marked (NASB) taken from the New American Standard Bible®, Copyright © 1960, 1962, 1963, 1968, 1971, 1972, 1973, 1975, 1977, 1995 by The Lockman Foundation. Used by permission. Scripture quotations marked (HCSB) are taken from the Holman Christian Standard Bible®, Copyright © 1999, 2000, 2002, 2003, 2009 by Holman Bible Publishers. Used by permission. Holman Christian Standard Bible®, Holman CSB®, and HCSB® are federally registered trademarks of Holman Bible Publishers. Scripture quotations marked (GW) are taken from GOD'S WORD®, © 1995 God's Word to the Nations. Used by permission of Baker Publishing Group. Scripture taken from The Voice™. Copyright © 2008 by Ecclesia Bible Society. Used by permission. All rights reserved. Scripture quotations marked (NKJV) taken from the New King James Version®. Copyright © 1982 by Thomas Nelson. Used by permission. All rights reserved. Scripture taken from the Modern English Version. Copyright © 2014 by Military Bible Association. Used by permission. All rights reserved.

ISBN: 978-1-4866-1352-6 Printed in Canada

Word Alive Press
131 Cordite Road, Winnipeg, MB R3W 1S1
www.wordalivepress.ca

MIX
Paper from
responsible sources
FSC
www.fsc.org FSC® C103567

Cataloguing in Publication may be obtained through Library and Archives Canada

Contents

Acknowledgements

I want to acknowledge and thank all my weekly Soul H2O readers. You're the reason I continue to write, blog, and stay up too late on Sunday nights! Okay, maybe the late Sunday nights have more to do with my time management issues than all of you, but the feedback you send through emails, social media, and blog comments touches my heart and inspires me. Knowing that what I write is helping you to face struggles in your lives and come out victoriously makes everything worth it. Thank you for sharing your journeys with me as I share mine with you. I pray that God continues to refresh you through the words He directs me to write. Let's stay connected and see what God will do!

Todd, I want to thank you for continually speaking life into me and encouraging me to pursue my God-given dreams. Your love and support means the world to me! Thanks for being my in-house editor. Love you.

To all my kids: Brandon, Morgan, Shelby, and Brandon. Thanks for allowing me to share snippets of our life together as I write my devotions. Shelby, thanks for being my other in-house and away-in-Florida editor. Brandon and Shelby I can't thank you enough for your design advice about the cover. I couldn't be happier with it now.

Daryl Dreidger of Cowlick Studios, thanks for creating another book cover I can be proud of and that captures the essence of the book.

Warren Benson, thanks for not giving up on me when I didn't meet the deadlines! Todd and I wouldn't be where we are today without your impact on our lives. You've helped us to dream big and chase after those dreams. Your faith in us has been instrumental to so much that God is doing in and through us. We're thankful to call you a friend.

Jen, Evan, and the Word Alive Press crew, thanks for always being so encouraging, kind, and helpful. You make the process of publishing the best it could be.

Stephen, of Stephen Woo Photography, thanks for your skills!

To the Living Water: God, I am ever thankful for Your continual supply that refreshes my spirit. The Water of Your Word sustains and satisfies me. May I stay true to the calling you've placed on my life to share refreshment with others.

 Join the community! Sign up on

takethe40daychallenge.com

for encouragement along the way!

Subscribers receive forty short, daily emails to coincide
with the messages in the devotions of either *Soul H2O*
or *Water in the Desert*, helping to build the habit of
personal daily devotions.

Just 10 Minutes a Day to Change Your Life!

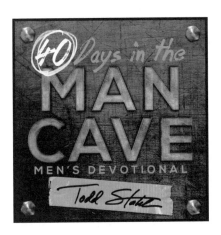

Know a guy who should take The 40-Day Challenge?
Meet the men's counterpart to the challenge:
40 Days in the Man Cave, by Todd Stahl!
Learn more at the back of this book.
www.takethe40daychallenge.com

Foreword

It's no coincidence that Sherry originally chose to release her Soul H2O devotionals on Monday mornings. There has been a real sense of them "setting the flow" for the week. More than once, I've marveled at how the theme, key verse, or even a poignant phrase has jumped right from the lines as I was reading. Spending time on Monday mornings reading the Soul H2O devotions is like having fellowship with a friend—Sherry, an authentic friend who dares to allow the Word to not only come alive but leap into the landscape of our lives!

And now we can read selected devotions in book form! These deliver that same refreshing cup of fellowship that her blog posts provide, not just with a friend but with the Father Himself. The Spirit reaches into the Word, and into the rich well that Sherry has allowed God to fill her with. Out of that double well come words that bring a life-sustaining and refreshing stream. The Lord promises to *"pour water on him who is thirsty"* (Isaiah 44:3, NKJV). Something will change when you just add water.

As you make your way through *Soul H2O*, you will not only read but you will receive. Life applications abound. Sherry has added to each devotion a section called "Drawing from the Well" which lists scriptures that will take you deeper. When we are dry and thirsty, everything else seems dry around us, too. But through this accumulation of daily fellowship with the Source, we will be both refreshed and strengthened to go back to the limitless well of our salvation and draw deeply for any and every situation (Isaiah 12:3). Sherry walks in that sensitivity to what God desires to say and do for herself and others. That's contagious! Get ready to be refreshed and become another source of refreshing to others.

—Rev. Peggy I. Kennedy
Author, international speaker
and cofounder of Two Silver Trumpets
www.TwoSilverTrumpets.ca

Introduction

This summer, I was able to spend a week at Braeside camp with my sister Lori's kids and my cousin Jen's kids. I forgot how fun it was to have little ones around! They're so full of life. One day we were all in the pool having a great time when Ella, my cousin's daughter, began splashing me. Jumping up and down, she giggled and splashed, giggled and splashed, all the time with a big smile on her face.

As I release this book, I feel just like Ella in the pool.

I pray that the overflow of my life splashes on you as you read the pages of this book. I'm asking the Lord to drench you in the Water of His Word. My heart's desire is that *Soul H2O* would be God's water supply to quench your spiritual thirst.

My hope is that the devotions I've written will whet your appetite for God's Word. I want to help you learn where to find your own source of refreshment, so I've added to each devotion a section called "Drawing from the Well" that includes four scriptures related to the topic. My words will hopefully bring inspiration, refreshment, and encouragement to your soul, but God's Word can change your life! This book is just a little stream leading you to the ocean!

So jump in, the water's just right!

DUE DATE

Humble yourselves, therefore, under God's mighty hand, that he may lift you up in due time.

—1 Peter 5:6

WHEN I WAS PREGNANT WITH MY SON BRANDON, THE doctor made me stop working a month and a half before the due date because I was in danger of preterm labor. The doctor knew that Brandon's best chance at a healthy life lay in prolonging his birth. I had to go in for weekly checkups, and every week they warned me about the situation. Days went by. Weeks went by. A month passed. Almost two months passed. By the time Brandon's due date came and went, I felt like I had been pregnant for two years! All this talk of an early delivery for months on end kept me ready for the birth, but it didn't happen. After the due date came and went, I wondered if he was ever coming out!

Finally, it happened. Labor pains began, and a baby was born!

Waiting for God's due date often involves a lot of waiting. You hear God's promise. Others confirm the promise and build your expectation of it. You see signs of it being fulfilled, and even a few false starts get your heart pumping! Then it seems like it's never going to happen. It's taking too long. Will it *ever* happen?

The beginning of Proverbs 13:12 says, *"Hope deferred makes the heart sick..."* When we've been hoping for something to be birthed for a long time and we don't see it happening, we get heartsick. We can lose hope and give in to discouragement.

The ending of Proverbs 13:12 explains that *"a longing fulfilled is a tree of life."* Just as surely as my son had a due date, so does your promise from God! Ecclesiastes 3:11 says, *"He has made everything beautiful in its time."* Your time will come. Your promise will come. God knows what's best for you and those around you. He knows what needs to take place so you'll be ready to take care of your promise. Trust Him with your due date!

PRAYER:

Father, today I humble myself before You. I put my life in Your mighty hand. Help me to trust You and believe that Your timing is best! May I know that You will bring to pass all that You have promised—on the perfect due date! In Jesus' name, amen.

DRAWING FROM THE WELL

- 1 Peter 5:6
- Proverbs 13:12
- Ecclesiastes 3:11
- Galatians 6:9

Christian Expectations

Dear friends, do not be surprised at the painful trial you are suffering, as though something strange were happening to you. But rejoice that you participate in the sufferings of Christ, so that you may be overjoyed when his glory is revealed.

—1 Peter 4:12–13

WE NEED TO CHANGE OUR CHRISTIAN EXPECTATIONS.

People tend to fall on one side of the fence or the other; some expect too much, yet others expect too little. There are strange folk (and I mean that in the nicest way) who spend their lives jumping from one side of the fence to the other. Those are the type of people this verse is talking about.

I have to watch it or I can be one of these strange fence-jumpers. I'll be sailing along believing God for great things, and then a problem hits and I'm tempted to fall into discouragement and give up hope. In my life, I have greatly struggled with getting-ready-for-the-carpet-to-be-pulled-out-from-under-me syndrome. It's an underlying fear of mine. Until recently, it was an unspoken mindset I functioned in—or should I say, *malfunctioned* in!

I believe part of my problem has been my Christian expectations. I have expected that problems won't get me because I do my best to live for God. It's illogical that I could read the Bible and arrive at this mindset. Illogical, yes, but a common Christian expectation!

This verse talks about the danger of becoming like the seed that falls on the rock, which falls away when trouble or persecution comes. We need to live our lives expecting the best yet not be shocked when trouble comes. We can trust that God will somehow turn it around for our best, using it for His glory! We need to expect that trials and suffering will come as much as we expect that God will bring us joy afterward. Living with this healthy Christian expectation will allow you to walk in confidence no matter your circumstances!

PRAYER:

Father, today I ask you to help me to increase my Christian expectations to a level that lines up with Your Word! Help me not jump the fence when trouble comes, but to stand in faith believing that when hardship hits I can trust You to bring joy back into my life. In Jesus' name, amen.

DRAWING FROM THE WELL

- 1 Peter 4:12–13
- Matthew 13:1–43 (the Parable of the Seeds)
- Psalm 30:5
- 2 Corinthians 4:17

To the Least of These

The King will reply, "I tell you the truth, whatever you did for one of the least of these brothers of mine, you did for me."

—Matthew 25:40

RECENTLY, SHELBY WENT AWAY TO COLLEGE. THERE ARE just so many things to get that we've had to find a few used pieces so we don't break the budget!

Shelby was given a shelf from Todd's cousin. She wanted to get it, paint it, and distress it, but she didn't know how. Todd surprised her for her birthday by refinishing and distressing the old shelf into a beautiful, new-looking shelf that matched her bed. She was thrilled! I told Todd that when he does nice things for my daughter, he's doing something nice for me. As soon as it came out of my mouth, I thought of Matthew 25:40, today's verse.

I heard this scripture often growing up. My grandma Pearl ran a ministry at my home church, Bethel Gospel Tabernacle in Hamilton. It started out with just a box at the back of our church to donate food for Christmas hampers and grew into a large, free, store-like portable at the back of our church property. It's now open year-round to provide for refugees, immigrants, single parents, families, or anyone else in need. The building is filled with groceries, clothes, and furniture to meet whatever needs arise. This ministry does so much for "the least of these."

At eighty-six, Gram passed away and the funeral home said they had never seen such an immense attendance for someone her age. About eight hundred people attended her funeral. People from many nations came and spoke about how Gram had blessed their lives and led them to Christ. Gram reminded us how we needed to help others when she quoted Matthew 25:40, but we heard this lesson louder through her actions.

I remember meeting a stranger at church as a teenager. She came to meet with my grandma and thank her for the impact Gram had made as her foster mother, and to let Gram know that she had given her life to Christ. The woman didn't know where my grandma lived these forty-odd years later, but she assumed correctly that she would find Gram at church.

I will never forget the stories Gram told of bringing groceries to people's houses and watching them break down crying, thanking God. Matthew 25:40 was the mandate of my grandmother's life, and she lived it out well!

So, what can you do to bring help to "the least of these"?

PRAYER:

Father, I thank You for all You have blessed me with. Help me to look beyond myself and search out those I could bless for You. May I be Your hands extended. In Jesus name, amen.

DRAWING FROM THE WELL

- Matthew 25:40
- Proverbs 14:31
- Proverbs 19:17
- Matthew 10:42

Repeats

...do not worry... do not worry... do not worry...
—Matthew 6:25, 31, 34

WHEN I WANT TO GET MY KIDS TO UNDERSTAND OR remember something, I repeat myself. The more important it is, or the more they ignore me, the more I'll repeat it. God, our heavenly father, does the same. As you study the Word of God, you need to take note of the repeats.

The verses in this portion of the Bible are so repetitive, and I mean that in a good way! I'm overwhelmed at how many times God encourages us in the Bible not to worry, not to be afraid, not to fear, and not to fret. Jesus sounds like a skipping record, repeating His message not to worry three times!

Most versions of the Bible translate these verses as "do not worry," but the Modern English Version uses the phrase "take no thought." As I contemplated this wording, it occurred to me that our brains are filled with countless random thoughts. We can choose which thoughts we will take and which ones we'll let pass through. Paul encourages us in 2 Corinthians 10:5 to *"take captive every thought to make it obedient to Christ."*

Choose today which thoughts you'll play on the record player of your mind. When worry hits the repeat button, move the needle and remind yourself of Jesus' words as He repeats "do not worry, do not worry, do not worry!"

PRAYER:

Father, thank You for giving me the ability to control my thoughts. When my worries override my thinking, help me to gain control and take captive every thought and make it obedient to Your Son. Because You're my Father, I don't need to worry. I place my trust in You. In Jesus' name, amen.

DRAWING FROM THE WELL

- Matthew 6:25–34
- 2 Corinthians 10:5
- Proverbs 3:5–6
- Philippians 4:6–7

Never

...the Lord your God goes with you; he will never leave you nor forsake you.

—Deuteronomy 31:6

I TAUGHT A LADIES' BIBLE STUDY GROUP WITH MY FRIENDS Julie and Michelle through my book, *Water in the Desert*. We worked so well as a team and loved working together. Then Michelle's husband got a job pastoring three hours away. It was a difficult loss for our group, but God brought along another amazing leader in a new friend, Erica. We began to work well together when my speaking schedule got really busy. I knew the Lord was directing me to step out of my comfort zone and leave my role as Bible study leader, but it was hard.

Leaving isn't something I ever wanted to do. I love being a part of a team and I felt a deep connection with the women we taught. This was my tribe, my girls, my friends. I never wanted to leave them. Going through these changes made me think about how God is the only one who can keep a promise to never leave you. Friends or family, no matter how well-meaning they are, cannot keep this promise at all times.

The Bible has so many records of God's promise to never leave us, but I think this message is best displayed for us as God reveals His stick-to-itiveness while leading the Israelites through the desert.

In order to direct the people to go the right way, and to display His presence, God placed before His people a pillar of cloud during the day and a pillar of fire at night. Never once did they leave their place. The cloud and fire were visual reminders that God was with them. They were never alone.

Today's verse tells us that God is with us. He *never* leaves, forsakes, rejects, or abandons us. How incredible is that? God so wants us to understand that He will never leave us that He sends this message to us at least ten times in His Word! Be encouraged today that God is with you and He's not going anywhere!

PRAYER:

Father, help me to let Your Word sink deep into my spirit so I can trust You. When You say that You're with me, it's true! Help me to be confident that You won't leave me, reject me, or abandon me. Let peace rise in my heart with the understanding of Your constant presence. In Jesus' name, amen.

DRAWING FROM THE WELL

Deuteronomy 31:6, 8, 23
Hebrews 13:5–6
1 Chronicles 28:20
Genesis 28:15

Wrong Way

*Your own ears will hear him. Right behind you a voice
will say, "This is the way you should go," whether to
the right or to the left.*

—Isaiah 30:21, NLT

WHEN I MARRIED TODD IN MY FORTIES, I MOVED THREE
hours away from where I had grown up to an area I had
only visited a few times. In the first two years after I
moved, I found myself lost and going the wrong way more
than I had in my entire life before. I used to know my way
around and hardly ever had to ask for directions. All that
changed when I moved to an area I wasn't familiar with!

How easily we can slip into a pattern like that. We can
get so used to things around us. We begin to feel like we
know the direction our lives should go, so we stop asking
God for directions and just keep going our own way. God is
so gracious and kind that He doesn't let us keep going the
wrong way forever. I take comfort in knowing that no matter if, or should I say when, I make a wrong turn, He'll be
right behind me, saying, "This is the way you should go."

Some of you reading this have ventured down a path
God didn't want you to walk on, so you need to be redi-
rected. Others are blazing new trails as God directs and yet

sometimes feel lost. Be comforted by another word from God in Isaiah 42:16:

> I will lead blind Israel down a new path, guiding them along an unfamiliar way. I will make the darkness bright before them and smooth out the road ahead of them. Yes, I will indeed do these things; I will not forsake them. (NLT)

Going the wrong way or just needing directions? Trust God to guide you in the way you should go!

PRAYER:

Father, today I thank You that You are good and that You don't leave us stranded. I appreciate Your grace and how You forgive me when I go my own way. Help me to listen for Your voice of direction and walk in Your ways. In Jesus' name, amen.

DRAWING FROM THE WELL

- Isaiah 30:21
- Isaiah 42:16
- Isaiah 48:17
- Psalm 32:8

Run to Win!

You've all been to the stadium and seen the athletes race. Everyone runs; one wins. Run to win. All good athletes train hard. They do it for a gold medal that tarnishes and fades. You're after one that's gold eternally.
—1 Corinthians 9:24–25, The Message

"HE SHOOTS, HE SCORES!" THAT'S A FAMILIAR SOUND IF YOU ever watch hockey on TV. Tonight I went to Brandon's hockey game. I was nervous when the other team scored first, but his team was playing to win—and win they did, with a final score of six to three. Three of those goals were assisted by Brandon! It was such an exciting game to watch because the boys were focused on winning to the very end.

Not so exciting are the games when the team gets behind and they give up. I know it frustrates Brandon. He strives to win in everything he does. As the captain of two hockey teams, he plays to win!

Life can be like a game of hockey. When we're gaining in life, it's easy to stay excited and focused on winning. We can be friendlier, happier, and take more chances when things are going well. It's harder to stay focused and keep that victory mentality when we fall behind. Our speed decreases, along with our ambition. Soon we've gone from full speed ahead to sitting on the bench.

Too many times, we take ourselves out of the game. We give up when we need to rally ourselves and exercise our hope because we serve the God of great comebacks! Just think of Calvary and what looked like sure defeat. Remember that Good Friday is followed by Easter Sunday and Christ's resurrection! God desires for you to win, and His Word assures it. So keep the faith and run to win!

PRAYER:

Father, thank You that when I put my faith in you, I will be an overcomer! Help me to not look at my circumstances, whether good or bad, but to trust in You and keep running to win so that I can one day receive the eternal prize You have for me! Thank You! In Jesus' name, amen.

DRAWING FROM THE WELL

- 1 Corinthians 9:24–25
- Philippians 3:12–14
- 2 Timothy 4:7
- Hebrews 12:1

Tough Tattoo

Be strong and courageous, because you will lead these people to inherit the land I swore to their forefathers to give them. Be strong and very courageous.

—Joshua 1:6–7

WHEN MY DAUGHTER SHELBY GRADUATED FROM HIGH school, her main grad gift from me was that I took her to get a tattoo. Call me a bad parent and say what you like, but this tattoo just had to be inked!

Shelby has wanted to get a tattoo of the Hebrew word for "endure" this past year. You see, graduating high school and getting this far in life hasn't been a cakewalk, and it doesn't seem like it's going to get much easier for a while. Recently, an oral surgeon put Shelby on a soft-food diet for two months! This will hopefully ward off the need for jaw surgery. I once heard someone say, "God wants us to do hard." I agree!

In today's verse, God was empowering Joshua by telling him he was going to lead these people to inherit the land, but it wasn't going to be a cakewalk for them either! They would have to endure many battles to fulfill all of God's plans for their lives. God had to keep reminding them to be strong and courageous.

I'm so proud of Shelby! Like Joshua and all the Israelites, she has learned to be an overcomer by living out this verse, and you can too!

PRAYER:

Father, thank You for giving me what it takes to endure! May I be strong and courageous in all that life throws at me, trusting that You will be with me all the way to the Promised Land! In Jesus' name, amen.

DRAWING FROM THE WELL

- Joshua 1:6–7
- Deuteronomy 1:21
- 2 Samuel 10:12
- 2 Timothy 1:7

Testing

The Lord blessed the latter part of Job's life more than the first.

—Job 42:12

IT'S A GOOD THING TESTS DON'T GO ON FOREVER! NO ONE would ever want to stay in school if there were tests every day. I loved how teachers threw parties at the end of each school year when I was young. Once you finished your tests and submitted all assignments, the fun began. Much like the teacher model, God has set a precedent in His Word that when you've successfully gone through a time of testing, it will be followed with a time of blessing. Whether it takes place here or in heaven, testing is followed by blessing!

There are so many biblical examples of this principle: Noah, Abraham, Joseph, Esther... the list could go on, but the biggest example is seen in the life of Job. In Job 1, we read the record of a conversation between God and the devil discussing how good Job is. God saw Job as faithful. The devil—which is literally translated as "the accuser"—accused Job of only being faithful to God because God had blessed him so much. The devil asked if he could test Job in the areas of his blessing, and God agreed. First the devil killed all of Job's servants, next all his children, and then all his livestock. This was the equivalent of financial and family ruin. After all these losses, Job still kept his faith in God.

The devil went to God again and asked if he could further test Job, and God agreed. The devil gave Job boils all over his body. Still Job remained faithful to God. It wasn't like he enjoyed it or was happy throughout it all—Job was very human in his response—but he never turned his back on God. Job cursed the day he was born, but still he did not curse God. Even when he lost everything and couldn't see any blessing, he still believed that God was good. What an incredible testimony!

At the end, we read about how God blessed Job with *more* than he had in the first part of his life. Job ended up with twice of what he'd owned before, and he'd already been a very wealthy man. God blessed Job with seven more sons and three daughters, giving him a long life so that he would see even his great-great-grandchildren live. When we look at the life of Job, we can be encouraged to stay faithful through trials because testing is followed by blessing!

PRAYER:

Father, I thank You that You see me as good even when the accuser talks differently. Help me to listen to what You say. Thank You that Your plans for me are good and that You won't let me be tempted beyond what I can bear. Help me to stand strong so I can pass the tests of my life and walk in Your blessing! In Jesus' name, amen.

DRAWING FROM THE WELL

- Job 1:8–12, Job 42
- Romans 2:11, Acts 10:34
- 1 Corinthians 10:13
- James 1:12

Rewards

And without faith it is impossible to please God, because anyone who comes to him must believe that he exists and that he rewards those who earnestly seek him.
—Hebrews 11:6

WHEN THINGS GO WRONG, OR WHEN THINGS GO RIGHT, MY husband Todd and I often quote the end part of this verse: "God rewards those who earnestly seek him." But until now, I never took the time to understand how the whole verse comes together.

Hebrews 11:6 tells us that we can't please God without faith. That means the reverse is also true: we *can* please God *with* faith. Which makes me ask, faith in what? The verse answers this question. If we want to please God, we need to believe two things. First, we must believe God exists. For some this is hard, because God is spirit and you can't see him with your natural eyes. Much like the wind, God isn't visible, but we can see how He affects things. Secondly, we must believe that He rewards those who earnestly seek Him—long before you ever see the reward!

When the bills are mounting and the problems are still around, you have to believe that God is going to reward you for seeking him. Hebrews 11:1 teaches that *"faith is being sure of what we hope for and certain of what we do not see.*" Be sure that our loving God will reward you. His Word promises it! Open your spiritual eyes to see the truth that God exists and have faith to believe that He rewards those who earnestly seek Him.

PRAYER:

Father, today I pray like the desperate dad in Mark 9:24: "*I do believe; help me overcome my unbelief!*" By a work of Your spirit, please give me the gift of faith to believe You will reward me as I seek You. Thank You in advance for all the blessings You're bringing into my life! In Jesus' name, amen.

DRAWING FROM THE WELL

- Hebrews 11:1, 6
- Jeremiah 31:16
- Mark 9:24
- Ruth 2:12

Backing Up Others

...Abram gave [him] the name Ishmael...

—Genesis 16:15

HAS GOD EVER SPOKEN TO YOU? HAGAR MUST HAVE TOLD Abram the story of God meeting her in the desert and all He spoke to her about the child she was going to have. You know how women can be... they go into great depth of detail recounting meetings like that! You can practically hear Hagar telling Abe how broken she was, how afraid for her life she was, how confused she was, how thirsty she had been in the desert, how lost she had been, how miraculously God had spoken to her, telling her that she was going to have a son named Ishmael. Abraham must have believed Hagar, as the Bible says, *"Abram gave [him] the name Ishmael."*

As a servant in their household, Hagar must have known about the promise of God over Abram's life to have a child and be the father of many nations. I would assume that Abraham and Hagar thought this child growing inside of her was how God was going to fulfill His promise. Hearing this obviously upset Sarah. Out of Sarah's hurt, she mistreated Hagar, causing her to run away. God met Hagar in the desert and spoke promises over her and her son-to-be, giving the child his name.

Abraham backed up what God told Hagar by naming their child Ishmael. He validated the call of God on Hagar and Ishmael by doing it. Just as a worship leader needs backup singers, we need people in our lives who, through their words and actions, support and validate what God has spoken to us.

Joseph and Elizabeth did this for Mary, Paul did this for Timothy, and Todd has done this for me! I have been blessed to have so many people speak and put action behind their words to back up what God has spoken to me.

The next time someone shares with you what God has spoken to them, take the time to listen. Affirm them and back up what God has set in motion. When you do, you'll become part of the miracle!

PRAYER:

Father, I thank You for the people You've put in my life to back me up. Help me to listen to them and not those who try to tear me down and distract me from what You are doing in my life. Help me to keep trusting in Your promise. In Jesus' name, amen.

DRAWING FROM THE WELL

- Genesis 16:15
- John 15:15
- Proverbs 17:17
- Proverbs 18:24

Internship

Looking at the man, Jesus felt genuine love for him. "There is still one thing you haven't done," he told him. "Go and sell all your possessions and give the money to the poor, and you will have treasure in heaven. Then come, follow me."

At this the man's face fell, and he went away sad, for he had many possessions.

—Mark 10:21–22, NLT

MY STEPDAUGHTER BECAME INVOLVED IN POLITICS DURING her last few years at university and realized a passion she didn't know she had. Morgan recognized that to enter into a political career, she needed to complete a government internship. She landed an amazing position as the summer intern for the Minister of Tourism, Culture, and Sport. She learned so much and was blessed to be a part of the successful 2015 Toronto Pan Am games. Morgan was willing to move four hours away from home and work two jobs in order to position herself one step closer to her dream.

The rich young ruler in the above scripture said he wanted to do whatever it took to gain eternal life. Jesus even offered him a personal internship, but he refused when he felt the cost to follow was too great.

His decision was a drastic contrast to the choice of Jesus' disciples. When Jesus found a group of fishermen out fishing, he called them and offered the same type of internship as He had offered to the rich man. The Bible tells it like this:

> Jesus called out to them, "Come, follow me, and I will show you how to fish for people!"
> —Mark 1:17, NLT

Immediately they left their nets and followed Him. The disciples' lives were forever changed as they followed Jesus.

The Bible is full of internship examples, like Moses and Joshua, Elijah and Elisha, Paul and Timothy, and Jesus and the disciples. So are you a Moses or a Joshua, a mentor or a disciple right now? There will always be mentors and people who need mentoring. You're wise to learn from godly direction, and a blessing when you lead others with all your heart.

PRAYER:

Father, I thank You for placing godly mentors in my life who help me grow into the person You've divinely designed me to be. Help me to discern what season I'm in and whether it's time for me to lead, learn, or do both at the same time. May I always stay registered in Your internship program! In Jesus' name, amen.

DRAWING FROM THE WELL

- Mark 10:20–21
- Exodus 24:13–18
- 1 Kings 19:16, 21, 2 Kings 2:1–2
- Mark 1:16–20

Unwavering Faith

But even if he does not...

—Daniel 3:18

I'VE ALWAYS LOVED THE STORY OF HOW SHADRACH, Meshach, and Abednego survived being thrown into a fiery furnace. If you went to Sunday school in the 70s, the song "Three Hebrew Boys," sung to the tune of "Three Blind Mice," is most likely running through your head now, and probably will be for the rest of the day! The song goes on to say, "But God delivered them out, you know... three Hebrew boys." Their miraculous protection from the fiery furnace would seem the most incredible part of the story, but to me, their unwavering faith, despite the outcome, is the most astounding detail.

When Nebuchadnezzar, king of Babylon, raged and told the three Hebrew boys how he was going to throw them into a blazing furnace, their response is what real faith is made of! These teenagers confidently stated that God was able to deliver them and how they thought He would. Next they made the boldest of faith statements, ending their declaration with *"But even if he does not... we will not serve your gods"* (Daniel 3:18). Their faith didn't hinge on whether God delivered them; it had nothing to do with their circumstances. The boys walked in and out of the furnace with unwavering faith.

When a friend of mine was diagnosed with Stage Four cancer, the news hit his relatives and our church family pretty hard. I was challenged at his and his wife's declaration of unwavering faith in God on Facebook. Just days after the diagnosis, they posted, "We trust in God's plans, even if the healing never comes and we are committed to using this season we have unexpectedly been thrown into to grow in our Faith further, despite the outcome." Such unwavering faith in a faithful God.

Today, look beyond your circumstances and let unwavering faith rise up in you!

PRAYER:

Father, I state my faith in Your ability to deliver me out of each and every circumstance. You are almighty. That means You hold all the power! You're all-knowing and always present. No matter what's going on, I'm not alone. You're in the fire with me. Please help me to exercise unwavering faith, no matter the outcome, all the days of my life. In Jesus' name, amen.

DRAWING FROM THE WELL

- Daniel 3:1
- Daniel 3:4–6
- Daniel 3:8–28
- Hebrews 10:39

Fearful Timidity vs. Godly Confidence

For God has not given us a spirit of fear and timidity, but of power, love, and self-discipline.
—2 Timothy 1:7, NLT

For God hath not given us the spirit of fear; but of power, and of love, and of a sound mind.
—2 Timothy 1:7, KJV

For God has not given us a spirit of fearfulness, but one of power, love, and sound judgment.
—2 Timothy 1:7, HCSV

WHEN MY CHILDREN WERE YOUNG, THEY STRUGGLED WITH fears, as many children do. When these episodes occurred, I often quoted this verse and had them memorize it. Many a nightmare ended with the comfort of this scripture.

As my kids grew older, I saw the dangers of allowing them to stay fearful and timid. Timidity brings on fear that prevents you from enjoying all that God has for your future. I wanted my kids to lay hold of the message that God had given them power, love, a sound mind, and the ability to be self-disciplined so they could live with godly confidence.

I looked up the dictionary meaning of timidity and became fixated on studying the list of its synonyms and antonyms. The synonyms are: fainthearted, fearful, fearsome, mousy, scary, skittish, shy, timorous, and tremulous.[1] Who wants to be all that? No wonder God said He did *not* give us the spirit of all those characteristics. No one grows up saying, "I want to be a mousy, skittish kind of person who's afraid of everything." No one wants that, and God doesn't want that for us either. So how do we break free of this timidity and gain godly confidence?

If I lived a life of godly confidence in His Spirit, what would it look like?

The antonyms will help us better understand the spirit God is offering to us. Here they are: adventuresome, adventurous, audacious, bold, daring, dashing, gutsy, hardy, venturesome, and venturous.[2] Now these are the words I want people to use when describing me, my children, and my children's children, should the Lord tarry!

As believers, you have the same Spirit that raised Jesus from the dead living in you! Today, access the Spirit of God and walk in the godly confidence you've been given!

---

1 *Merriam-Webster*, "Timid." Date of access: March 23, 2015 (http://www.merriam-webster.com/dictionary/timid).
2 Ibid.

PRAYER:

Father, I thank You for the truth of your Word! Thank You that it's true whether I feel it or not. Help me to live free of fear and timidity. Help me to access Your spirit for power and love so that I may use self-discipline to walk in sound mind, using sound judgment! May I walk in godly confidence! In Jesus' name, amen.

DRAWING FROM THE WELL

- 2 Timothy 1:7
- 2 Corinthians 3:5–6
- Romans 8:11
- Romans 8:15

Payback or Reward?

The faithless will be fully repaid for their ways, and the good man rewarded for his.

—Proverbs 14:14

EVER SINCE STORES STARTED COMING OUT WITH REWARDS programs, my wallet has started getting thicker. I had to buy a separate card holder just to hold them all! Even though I don't like the added weight to my purse, I love all these programs—especially when they're free! It's so nice to get to the checkout and have the cashier ask if I want to use my points to pay for the purchase. Who wouldn't choose that? Stores reward us for shopping with them. God rewards us for the way we live.

Merriam-Webster describes the word payback as "punishment for something that was done in the past."[3] There's a strange website—www.thepayback.com—that's dedicated to recording payback stories of revenge. The funniest one I read was about a girl who played a payback prank on a cheating boyfriend by giving him a pair of box-

---

3 *Merriam-Webster*, "Payback." Date of access: March 24, 2015 (http://www.merriam-webster.com/dictionary/payback).

ers rubbed in poison ivy—before she told him she knew about his affair! Now that's one sassy lassy!

Without the grace of God in our lives, we would all reap the payback for our sins. Through Christ's work on the cross we receive His righteousness for free! We're rewarded with salvation and all His eternal blessings.
Payback or reward? It's your choice. But like I said, who wouldn't choose a reward?

PRAYER:

Father, I thank You for Your grace, which frees me from the law of the payback. May I continue to place my faith in You so that I may receive every reward You have for me here on earth and in heaven. In Jesus' name, amen.

DRAWING FROM THE WELL

- Proverbs 14:14
- Isaiah 61:8–9
- Hebrews 11:6
- 1 Timothy 4:16

Finding Christ?

Then Moses cried out to the Lord, and the Lord showed him a piece of wood. He threw it into the water, and the water became sweet.

—Exodus 15:25

Have you ever gone through a trying time and wondered where God was? Well, I have, and so did the Israelites. Today's scripture comes just after the Israelites crossed through the Red Sea. They had broken free of bondage in victory only to wander for three days without water!

They finally found water and ran off to drink it, but the water was bitter and undrinkable. That was enough suffering to make the people forget the Red Sea miracle and want to go back to their old lives. They grumbled and complained to Moses, who then did the right thing and cried out to the Lord. If only we took the time to cry out to the Lord like Moses did and wait for Him to speak! Oh, how different our lives would be!

God showed Moses a piece of wood. Moses threw it into the water, starting a chemical reaction that changed the whole body of water. Seriously? A piece of wood? This doesn't make sense, unless you see the cross symbolism. A piece of wood couldn't change water in the natural. God supernaturally used that piece of wood as a foreshadowing of the cross. Only Jesus can take the bitter sufferings we face and bring something sweet out of them. We need God to open our spiritual eyes so we can see that Christ is right there, just like the wood, mighty to save.

Moses took the time to cry out to God and ask Him to be involved in his problem. He expected God to show up, and show up He did! God provided sweet-tasting water in the desert. Take time today to bring your needs before God. Open your spiritual eyes to see Christ in your bitter circumstances and allow Him to give you sweet water!

PRAYER:

Father, You see the bitterness of life on this earth and stand along the sidelines waiting for me to tag you in. Open my eyes today to see You working on my behalf! May I never doubt that You are there, because You are. You are mighty to save! Thank You! In Jesus' name, amen.

DRAWING FROM THE WELL

- Exodus 15:25
- Jeremiah 29:13
- Matthew 7:7
- Deuteronomy 4:29

Forgiveness and Restored Relationship

*Be kind and compassionate to one another, forgiving
each other, just as in Christ God forgave you.*
—Ephesians 4:32

LIFE IS SO GENEROUS TO GIVE US LOTS OF OPPORTUNITIES
to extend forgiveness to people who hurt us. What's the
proper response to offence? Do we always have to forgive?
Does forgiveness equal restored relationship?

If we are to follow God's example, as this verse in-
structs us, then forgiveness is a must and restored relationships need to be our intent. Sadly, I don't think forgiveness
can always lead to restored relationships, and we see that in
Jesus' relationship with the Pharisees.

Isaiah 59:2 explains that our sin is an offence to God,
separating us in our relationship with Him. The more we
sin and the longer we continue offending Him, the more
distant our relationship with Him becomes. Forgiveness
can take place in an instant when a prayer is whispered,
but it takes time to rebuild a relationship with God. Restoration happens when we take ownership of our offence
and change our ways. We have to go through a process to
rebuild our closeness with the Father.

The same principle needs to be applied to our earthly relationships. We must forgive others for their offences towards us. If we don't, it keeps us bound in bitterness. It's healthy to learn that a restored relationship is separate from forgiveness and requires a healing process.

When approaching relationship restoration, we need to consider the whole counsel of scripture. Proverbs 4:23 warns, *"Guard your heart above all else, for it determines the course of your life"* (NLT). Proverbs 22:24 cautions, *"Do not make friends with a hot-tempered person, do not associate with one easily angered..."* Sometimes you'll need to forgive and protect yourself from unhealthy or even toxic relationships. In the best of times, forgiveness leads to a better, stronger restored relationship.

PRAYER:

Father, I thank You for Your forgiveness. I ask for grace to forgive others in my life who have hurt and offended me. I take myself out of the judge's seat and release them to Your judgement and justice. Please help me to guard my heart, without closing it in the area of relationship restoration. May I walk in Your wholeness. In Jesus' name, amen.

DRAWING FROM THE WELL

- Ephesians 4:32
- Isaiah 59:2
- Proverbs 22:24–25
- Proverbs 4:23

God of the Turnaround!

I'll turn things around for you. I'll bring you back...
You can count on it.

—Jeremiah 29:14, The Message

I THINK MY FAVORITE PART OF WATCHING THE OLYMPICS IS hearing about the athletes' journeys to the top of their game. There's something about a great turnaround story that gives me hope, especially when I seem to have lost my own.

So many times in life, I couldn't see how my life could turn around. How God could take my mess and turn it into a message? At times, all I saw was brokenness and heartache, yet I had an underlying trust in my Heavenly Father to bring about change for the better.

When Jeremiah spoke the words recorded in today's scripture, the people of Israel felt like I sometimes do. They couldn't see how God's promises to bless their nation could ever happen. They were in bondage—again. They had been caught in the cycle of *sin, slavery, sorrow, and salvation* for centuries. How could things ever change for them? Over and over, they seemed to get themselves back in the same trouble.

The key to breaking free is found in Jeremiah 29:13. Through Jeremiah, God tells His people, *"When you come looking for me, you'll find me... when you get serious about finding me... you won't be disappointed"* (The Message). When the Israelites turned to God and away from their sin, God broke them out of the cycle and brought them into the Promised Land!

Our Father is the God of the turnaround! The Bible is full of turnaround examples, from the nation of Israel to Joseph, Esther, David, Paul, and you can't forget Jesus. The Bible records these stories to build your hope and expectation that God can do it for you, because He can! Believe today that He is working behind the scenes to reveal Himself as Your God of the turnaround!

PRAYER:

Father, I thank You that You are all-powerful. Nothing is too hard for You! No problem is too difficult for You to break me free from. Help me to look for you today and stand on Your Word, trusting You for the turnaround in my life! Thank You! In Jesus' name, amen.

DRAWING FROM THE WELL

- Jeremiah 29:13–14
- Deuteronomy 30:3, 5
- Psalm 14:7, 126:4
- Matthew 28:5–6

Perfume and the Ice Bucket Challenge

*While Jesus was in Bethany in the home of a man
known as Simon the Leper, a woman came to him with
an alabaster jar of very expensive perfume, which she
poured on his head as he was reclining at the table.*
—Matthew 26:6–7

IN THE SUMMER OF 2014, YOU COULDN'T GO ON YOUR
computer or TV without seeing something about the Ice
Bucket Challenge! It was a far-reaching phenomenon that
went around the globe. All proceeds went to support amyo-
trophic lateral sclerosis (ALS). As a result of the challenge,
the ALS Association's website reported,

*The ALS Association has received $70.2 million in do-
nations compared to $2.5 million during the same time
period last year (July 29 to August 24). These donations have come from existing donors and 1.3 million
new donors to The Association.[4]*

---

4 *ALS Association*, "Ice Bucket Challenge Donations Reach $70.2 Mil-
lion." Date of access: March 25, 2015 (http://www.alsa.org/news/media/
press-releases/ice-bucket-donations-082414.html).

Most people spoke positively about the campaign, but sadly there were a few negative voices. Shockingly, Maclean's had an article condemning the Ice Bucket Challenge as a "marketing gimmick," "slaktivism," and went so far as to say it is "bad for you" to donate to a cause in this manner. The writer proposed that ALS had enough funds and didn't deserve this much investment compared to other diseases.[5] I can't imagine that he ever watched someone live and die with ALS. My college roommate's dad passed away from this horrible disease years ago. He went from being a strong carpenter to a shadow of himself through all the debilitating stages until it took his life.

When I hear any story, it often makes me think of a similar Bible story or verse. Reading the Maclean's article brought to my mind the incident when a woman poured expensive perfume on Jesus' head. The disciples scoffed and tried to sound all spiritual, saying that she was wasting her money and should have given the value of the perfume to the poor. Too quickly we can negatively judge a person's actions. Jesus reprimanded the disciples and said that the woman had done a beautiful thing.

Whenever we give of ourselves in time or money to help others, we can rest assured that our Heavenly Father

---

5 *Maclean's*, "Why the Ice Bucket Challenge Is Bad for You." Date of access: March 24, 2015 (http://www.macleans.ca/society/health/why-the-ice-bucket-challenge-is-bad-for-you/)

is pleased. From oil to ice buckets of water poured on the head, God sees it all as a beautiful thing!

PRAYER:

Father, help me to look for ways I can give to ease someone else's burden and bring You glory! May I take up the challenge to bless the lives of others. In Jesus' name, amen.

DRAWING FROM THE WELL

- Matthew 26:6–7
- John 12:2–4
- 2 Kings 4:8–10
- 1 Corinthians 10:31

God Doesn't Make Junk

For we are God's workmanship, created in Christ Jesus to do good works, which God prepared in advance for us to do.

—Ephesians 2:10

MY DAUGHTER SHELBY WATCHED A SHOW ABOUT PLASTIC surgeries gone wrong, and I couldn't help but join her. So many people struggling with self-esteem choose to go under the knife so they can feel better about themselves. I know there's nothing wrong with people choosing to have plastic surgery, but too often it starts and ends with an unhealthy mindset that they aren't made well, leaving them with an even more diminished self-worth. I guess no one has ever read them this verse and explained to them that God doesn't make junk!

You are God's handiwork. You are created by God and fashioned by His hand. Think about that. God, who is perfect, made *you!* God doesn't make junk. We know from the creation story that everything God creates is good, but when God creates people He says that they are *very* good! You are made *very* good, no matter what anyone says, or how you feel.

When we have an unhealthy view of ourselves, it affects every area of our lives. If the enemy can get us believing we weren't made well, he can sidetrack us from our purpose in life. We'll be focused on fixing ourselves instead of fulfilling the good works God has prepared for us to do. Believe who God says you are and you will fulfill the destiny He has prepared for you!

PRAYER:

Father, help me to see myself the way You see me. Thank You for creating me the way You did. Help me to see the greatness You have placed inside me so that I may live to do all You have prepared in advance for me to accomplish. In Jesus' name, amen.

DRAWING FROM THE WELL

- Ephesians 2:10
- Ephesians 1:6
- Genesis 1:31
- Psalm 139:13–14

Follow Me

There remains, then, a Sabbath-rest for the people of God; for anyone who enters God's rest also rests from his own work, just as God did from his.
        —Hebrews 4:9–10 (emphasis added)

Does the idiom "Do as I say, not as I do" annoy anyone else? It bothers me when I hear parents repeat this to their kids. They say it as if it's a joke, when really it's backed up by their actions. The Free Dictionary describes the phrase this way: "Take my advice, even though I am acting contrary to it."[6] I'm so thankful that we serve a Heavenly Father who doesn't parent like that! God never requires something of us that He hasn't modeled, like when He tells us to take a Sabbath rest, following His example.

Good leaders lead by example, not by rule. God the Father and His Son Jesus both led by example.

---

6 *The Free Dictionary*, "Do as I say, not as I do." Date of access: March 17, 2015 (http://idioms.thefreedictionary.com/Do+as+I+-say,+not+as+I+do).

> *"Come, follow me," Jesus said, "and I will make you*
> *fishers of men."*
>
> —Matthew 4:19

Jesus had every right to say "Follow me," because that's exactly what He was doing: fishing for people.

Paul encouraged believers many times to follow his example, even saying twice that people should "imitate" him. In Philippians 3:17, Paul said,

> *Join together in following my example, brothers and sisters, and just as you have us as a model,* keep your eyes on those who live as we do. (emphasis added)

We need to be Christians who lead by example, so that we can say, "Do as I say *and* as I do!"

PRAYER:

Father, I thank You for modeling good things before me. Help me to follow Your example to rest and model what I say, in what I do. May I live a life that will help others to be better if they follow after me. In Jesus' name, amen.

DRAWING FROM THE WELL

- Hebrews 4:9–10
- Matthew 4:19
- Philippians 3:17
- Philippians 1:27

Absolute Dependence

There remains, then, a Sabbath-rest for the people of God; for anyone who enters God's rest also rests from his own work, just as God did from his.

—Hebrews 4:9–10

WHY IS STRIKING A BALANCE BETWEEN WORK AND REST SO hard? It seems few people can master this balance. One person who nailed it, and helped countless others do the same, was Mary Kay Ash. Our society calls people like her "self-made," but I don't think that's how she would have described herself. Mary Kay's motto was "God first, family second, and career third." It remains the motto of her abundantly successful cosmetic company to this day.

When she started her company, May Kay Ash was a single mom by divorce and widowhood. Instead of trying to do it all on her own, she emphatically stated her absolute dependence on God to manage her company and her life.

In yesterday's devotion, we talked about living a life that's worth following, and Mary Kay fits the bill! Let's follow her lead and let the verses below strengthen our resolve for complete dependence on God to meet *all* our needs.

And this same God who takes care of me *will sup-ply* all *your needs from his glorious riches, which have been given to us in Christ Jesus.*

—Philippians 4:19, NLT (emphasis added)

And God is able *to bless you abundantly, so that in* all *things at all times, having* all *that you need, you will abound in* every good work.

—2 Corinthians 9:8 (emphasis added)

PRAYER:

Father, I thank You that I can rest because You will take care of me! Help me to live in absolute dependence on Your provision. In Jesus' name, amen.

DRAWING FROM THE WELL

- Hebrews 4:9–10
- Philippians 4:19
- 2 Corinthians 9:8
- Ephesians 3:20

Obedient Faith... Brings Rest

Therefore, since the promise of entering his rest still stands, let us be careful...

—Hebrews 4:1

WHY IS IT SO FUNNY WHEN OTHERS WIPE OUT? I LOVE THE TV show where everyone competes to finish a race without falling, but wiping out is inevitable. You can see the fall coming before they do!

Hebrews talks about how the Israelites are an example to us. Just like watching the TV show *Wipeout*, you can either learn from reading about the Israelites' mistakes, or you can make your own. Disobedience and lack of faith in God took away their rest. Obedience and faith are the keys that will open the door to your rest. No more striving to do enough, have enough, or be good enough. Simple obedience to God in faith is all it takes to enter into His rest.

When I hear the word obedience, I immediately think of a set of rules. It seems to me that God isn't describing rules in Hebrews 3–4. God's talking about living in obedience to who He's designed you to be, and following where He's destined you to go. To live out your purpose, you need faith—faith to believe in *who* God says *you* are and faith to believe that *He* will accomplish it *through you*.

When you're obedient to God's calling on your life, you're most at rest. No more striving to do enough, have enough, or be good enough. It's simple: obedient faith believes in what God says over your circumstances. That, my friend, brings rest!

PRAYER:

Father, help me to see the difference between striving and being at rest to follow You in obedient faith. Help me to believe in Your Word above all my thoughts, experiences, and circumstances. I declare my obedient faith to Your call. May I live in the rest You promise! In Jesus' name, amen.

DRAWING FROM THE WELL

- Hebrews 4:1
- Acts 3:19
- 2 John 1:6
- Luke 23:56

Keeping the Promise

> *On the plains of Moab by the Jordan across from Jericho the Lord said to Moses, "Speak to the Israelites and say to them: 'When you cross the Jordan into Canaan, drive out all the inhabitants of the land before you. Destroy all their carved images and their cast idols, and demolish all their high places. Take possession of the land and settle in it, for I have given you the land to possess.'"*
> —Numbers 33:50–53

I'M TRYING TO IMAGINE HOW THE ISRAELITES FELT WHEN they heard this direction from the Lord. I can see them saying, "I have to do what? Don't you know we just got out of the dry, difficult desert? Shouldn't we be on easy street now?"

Once in the Promised Land, the Israelites had to continue battling nations that opposed them. We have to stop being shocked that it isn't all sunshine and rainbows once we *get* our promise. The battle we had to fight to get our promise is sometimes easier than the battle to *keep* our promise, but there will be blessings to balance out the hardship.

Think of David's life and the progression of enemies he had to face—the lion, the bear, Goliath, Saul, and Absalom. At first you would think the biggest battle he had to face was Goliath, but I think having to repeatedly stand up against Saul, and then having his son as an enemy, were far worse than a nine-foot giant he never knew. His last battles were those closest to his heart.

When new struggles come our way, we can't quit. We need the tenacity that the writer of Hebrews described when he wrote,

> *So do not throw away your confidence; it will be richly rewarded. You need to persevere so that when you have done the will of God, you will receive what he has promised.*
>
> —Hebrews 10:35–36

To keep your promise, you need to live out the words of Winston Churchill and "Never, never, never give up!"

PRAYER:

Father, I thank You that You are with me. You give me what I need to face every enemy that comes against me. Help me push forward to take hold of and keep the promise You have for me. In Jesus' name, amen.

DRAWING FROM THE WELL

- Numbers 33:50–53
- Hebrews 10:35–36
- Galatians 6:9
- Psalm 126:5

Victory

So do not throw away your confidence; it will be richly rewarded. You need to persevere so that when you have done the will of God, you will receive what he has promised.

—Hebrews 10:35–36

YESTERDAY'S DEVOTION ENDED WITH TODAY'S VERSE AND a quote from Winston Churchill. Reading the quote by Churchill led me to research his life. He was such an inspiring man in a potentially depressing time.

In 1941, while World War II was raging and Europe was being held captive by a murderous madman, "Victor de Laveleye, former Belgian Minister of Justice and director of the Belgian French-speaking broadcasts on the BBC"[7] encouraged Belgians to form their hands into the V shape to represent victory. Months later, Winston Churchill began using the V sign in a speech. For four more years, through great tribulation and much defeat, Churchill continued to use this hand sign to address the people of England. This

---

7 Wikipedia, "V Sign." Date of access: March 24, 2015 (http://en.wikipedia.org/wiki/V_sign).

was a visual sign of his confidence in their victory. To their enemy, it was also a visual defiance and a clear message of their perseverance as a nation.

The character trait that most impressed me about Churchill was his optimism. Churchill impacted a nation to not throw away their confidence and persevere on their way to victory. Let this same mindset be yours. Signal to your enemy that you will endure until victory is achieved and you receive *all* that God has promised!

PRAYER:

Father, may a spirit of confidence in Your promises sweep over my spirit so I can persevere through anything the enemy throws my way. Help me to signal confidence and victory that will inspire others around me to great faith! In Jesus' name, amen.

DRAWING FROM THE WELL

- Hebrews 10:35–36
- Genesis 17:5
- Romans 4:17-18
- Ephesians 3:12

Fight the Urge to Repeat

When you see the ark of the covenant of the Lord your God, and the priests, who are Levites, carrying it, you are to move out from your positions and follow it. Then you will know which way to go, since you have never been this way before.

—Joshua 3:3–4

JUST BECAUSE TWO PEOPLE HAVE THE SAME PROBLEM doesn't mean God's solution is the same.

The Israelites were again at a place where they had to cross a raging body of water to break free. To some it might have looked like they had been in this same situation before, but God was telling them it was different. He said that they had *never* been there before. Moses got into trouble when he tried to solve the problem the same way as he had when the people had been crying out for water in the desert. Moses took time to ask God what to do, but he ignored the directions God gave him. God instructed Moses to speak to the rock and water would gush out. Instead, Moses struck the rock like he had done before. The choice to repeat instead of follow cost Moses the right to enter the Promised Land.

God's desire is that we be in relationship with Him. He wants us to consult Him and spend enough time with Him so we know what His direction is for each of our lives. He doesn't want us to assume we know what to do, even if we've *"been this way before."* So, fight the urge to repeat and ask God what He wills for you today!

PRAYER:

Father, I want to thank You for speaking. I'm so glad You're alive and able to direct me where I need to go. Help me to always ask for Your direction and follow Your lead! In Jesus' name, amen.

DRAWING FROM THE WELL

- Joshua 3:3–4
- Exodus 17:3–6
- Numbers 20:7–12
- Isaiah 43:18–19

Prepare the Way

Consecrate yourselves, for tomorrow the Lord will do amazing things among you.

—Joshua 3:5

TOO MANY PEOPLE DON'T GET TO SEE THE AMAZING THINGS God has planned for them because they don't get ready in advance. Sometimes we have a movie theatre attitude. We want to just sit back, relax, and watch the show when God asks us to perform vital roles. Life is not a spectator sport. God desires to partner with us to see His plans and purposes for our lives released.

When the Israelites were crossing over the Jordan River into the Promised Land, God required that they consecrate themselves. They had to do it, not God. Their acts of consecration were a sign that they were dedicating their lives for a sacred purpose. God promised them that if they did this, He would follow up by doing amazing things among them—and He sure did stick to His Word! After they consecrated themselves, God parted the flood-stage waters of the Jordan River and let them walk across on dry ground. Then God caused the walls of Jericho to crumble as the Israelites marched and worshipped around them. How amazing is that?

Why did all these miracles take place? Because God's people prepared themselves in advance. During the hard times, while still in the desert, they lived out the words of Isaiah 40:3, which says,

> In the wilderness, *get it ready! Prepare the way; make it a straight shot. The Eternal would have it so. Straighten the way in the wandering desert to make the crooked road wide and straight for our God.* (The Voice, emphasis added)

Get ready in your desert times and you'll be preparing the way for God to amaze you!

PRAYER:

Father, thank You for Your power to do amazing things in my life! Help me to prepare the way in my heart so You'll have a roadway into my life for the miraculous! In Jesus' name, amen.

DRAWING FROM THE WELL

- Joshua 3:5
- Exodus 19:10-11
- Isaiah 40:3
- Matthew 3:3

DEVOTION 28:

It Ain't Always Easy

*Choose twelve men from among the people, one from
each tribe, and tell them to take up twelve stones from
the middle of the Jordan from right where the priests
stood and to carry them over with you and put them
down at the place where you stay tonight... to serve as
a sign among you... These stones are to be a memorial
to the people of Israel forever.*

—Joshua 4:2–3, 6–7 (emphasis added)

I once saw a counselor who said, "If God asks you
to cross the road, you can bet there'll be a parade on the
street." God's plan is often simple, but not always easy!

The Israelites didn't know easy! To me, this request
from God in Joshua 4 was the most difficult step in the
desert exodus to the Promised Land. At first all they had to
do was dip their toes in the Jordan River; then God parted
the waters for them to walk across on dry ground with a
strong wind. Scripture tells us that the river was at flood
stage. A rushing river and strong winds would make for a
scary crossing!

I would think the priests' first thought would have
been to get to the other side and away from danger, but after the crossing twelve men had to go back into the middle

of the parted river and pick out twelve stones. Research suggests that the river would have been about 360 feet wide where they crossed. To give you some perspective, that's the distance of an NFL football field, with raging water heaped up on either side! Gulp. Take a deep breath, and go back in there, boys! Imagine the faith they had to muster up to fulfill the task God called them to. They probably were thinking, "This is stupid. It doesn't make sense. What difference is it going to make if I get a stone and we pile them up? Why is God making us do this?"

How many times do we question God like this?

The priests had no way of knowing how many sermons and books would be written about their heroic task; no idea that their seemingly unimportant step of faith would motivate others for centuries. It ain't always easy, but take that step of faith, no matter how difficult, and follow God today. You'll never know how many people's lives you will inspire!

PRAYER:

Father, I thank You for all the examples You give in Your Word that let me see real people living out real faith. Help me to go beyond the easy and press forward to what You've called me to do. Let me not shrink back when things get difficult but accomplish what You've called me to do so that others will be inspired. In Jesus' name, amen.

DRAWING FROM THE WELL

- Joshua 4:2–3, 6–7
- Hebrews 10:23
- Deuteronomy 5:33
- 2 Thessalonians 3:5

Ask, Don't Assume

And when the Israelites heard that they had built the altar...the whole assembly of Israel gathered... to go to war against them.

—Joshua 22:11–12

TEXTING IS BOTH THE BEST AND WORST INVENTION OF THE century. How often are texts read with the wrong message being received on the other end? We can read them with the wrong tone and misunderstand what the sender was trying to say. Autocorrect makes our lives even more confusing! When it comes to texting, we would be better off to ask questions before assuming the worst!

The Israelites sort of followed the "ask, don't assume" motto. After they entered into the Promised Land, two and a half tribes settled on the far side of the Jordan River, by choice. They're known today as the trans-Jordan tribes, and they immediately built an imposing altar big enough that it could either be seen across the river or was such a spectacle that it became all the talk.

Somehow, the other nine and a half Israelite tribes found out. They assumed that their relatives had left the faith and built an altar to another god. Infuriated, they were ready to go to war against them. Thankfully, they sent over tribal leaders to check out what was going on before sending the army. Instead of asking, though, they began telling off the trans-Jordan tribes for leaving the faith and building the altar. How embarrassed they must have been when they finally let their brothers explain and found out that they'd built the altar as a memorial to God for bringing them there. Their discussions brought the truth to light and strengthened all the tribes' relationships with each other.

Learn another lesson from watching the Israelites do it right and wrong. The next time someone upsets you, before you let your mind go crazy... ask, don't assume!

PRAYER:

Father, thank You for being with me in every circumstance of life. Please help me to control my thoughts and ask before I assume the worst. I need Your help to wisely discern the situations of my life. In Jesus' name, amen.

DRAWING FROM THE WELL

- Joshua 22:11–12
- Philippians 4:6
- Luke 11:9
- John 16:24

Contentment that Leads to Freedom

...I have learned to be content whatever the circumstances... I have learned the secret of being content in any and every situation...

—Philippians 4:11–12

For I can do everything through Christ, who gives me strength.

—Philippians 4:13 (NLT)

ONE OF MY FAVORITE CHILDHOOD MEMORIES FROM Disney World was climbing up the Swiss Family Robinson treehouse! I was mesmerized by all the inventions that helped them survive. The Disney movie and TV series were both adaptations of the book *Robinson Crusoe*, a story which inspired many other books, films, plays—and clearly Walt Disney! In the original book, Robinson ends up shipwrecked on a deserted island. He finds a Bible inside one of the pirate chests. Reading the Word changes his life! As he reads, he begins to accept his situation and makes the most of his circumstances. Amazingly, after coming to peace while living in difficult times, God blesses Robinson and provides a way out. He eventually breaks free of his captivity and returns to his homeland of England.

Paul writes about how he *learned* to be content. It does *not* come naturally! Well, at least not to me! Hebrews 13:5 says to *"be content with what you have, because God has said, 'Never will I leave you; never will I forsake you.'"* True contentment comes when we learn, like Paul and Robinson Crusoe, that God is with us no matter what desert or deserted island we face. When we're at peace in the middle of the storm, that's when victory comes—and freedom is always close behind!

PRAYER:

Father, thank You for all that I have. Help my desires not to get out of line and lead me away from You. Help me to live truly content, enjoying the freedom that brings! In Jesus' name, amen.

DRAWING FROM THE WELL

- Philippians 4:11–13
- Luke 3:14
- 1 Timothy 6:6–8
- Hebrews 13:5

Rainbows and Lightning

*Without warning, a furious storm came up on the lake,
so that the waves swept over the boat. But Jesus was
sleeping.*

—Matthew 8:24

SHELBY SHOWED ME AN AMAZING INSTAGRAM PHOTO OF
double rainbows beside a lightning bolt. The contrasting
imagery spoke to me about life with God. Even when we're
in the middle of a storm, God has a promise for us! In Genesis 9:13, God said, *"I will put my rainbow in the clouds to be a
sign of my promise to the earth"* (GW). In life, we can have at
the same time promises and storms, rainbows and lightning.

I've always loved the story about Jesus in the boat with
His disciples. These guys were following God's direction
for their lives when a storm came without warning. It was
such a crazy storm that the waves crashed over the boat.
The Bible says, *"But Jesus was sleeping."* What? Sleeping
in a storm like that? Jesus was experiencing rainbows and
lightning, but all the disciples could see was the storm. In a
panic, the disciples woke Jesus up and begged Him to save
them. Did they really think Jesus was going to let them
drown? When Jesus got up, He rebuked the disciples for
their lack of faith. He rebuked the wind and the waves to

bring everyone onboard with the peace He had. The Bible records that the disciples were amazed and seemed shocked that Jesus had the power to calm the storm. Too often we're like the disciples and forget to stand on the promises He's given in the midst of life's storms.

Today, ask God to show you His rainbow in the midst of your lightning. Speak the truth of His promises to your storm and watch the clouds part.

PRAYER:

Father, I thank You for peace. Help me to understand your promises and speak them out when storms arise. May I walk in faith, no matter the weather! In Jesus' name, amen.

DRAWING FROM THE WELL

- Matthew 8:24
- Genesis 9:13
- John 14:27
- John 16:33

The Closeness of God

They will be my people, and I will be their God.
—Jeremiah 32:38

ISN'T IT AMAZING HOW THE MORE YOU LOVE SOMEONE, THE closer you want to get to them? It's this desire for intimate relationship that propels men to cross over the commitment line and get married. It's out of God's desire for intimate relationship with the people He created that He crossed over the commitment line and actively pursued friendship with us!

At the beginning of the Bible, we can read how God came down and hung out with Adam and Eve in the garden. God originally created mankind to have fellowship with Him and even went so far as to create the perfect place to fellowship with us. Sadly, sin messed that all up.

In Exodus 25:8, God gives instructions on how to build the Ark of the Covenant. The Ark was to be a symbol of God's presence among His people. The priests were to put the testimony—the record of God's laws and promises—inside the Ark. God wanted to make it clear in Exodus 25:8 that His every intention was to live close to His people: *"Then have them make a sanctuary for me, and I will dwell among them."*

As time passed, God desired to come even closer in relationship with us. Jesus came down to earth to live among us full-time. Even that didn't satisfy God's desire for relationship. He wanted more; He wanted closer.

In John 16:7, Jesus tells the people that it would be better for Him to go so that the Counselor, the Holy Spirit, could come. The Holy Spirit then came so that God could dwell in us! 1 Corinthians 3:16 tells us that we are God's temples, His place of fellowship with others, and that God's Spirit dwells *in* us.

God desires to grow closer in relationship with you! Will you let Him in?

PRAYER:

Father, through the power of the Holy Spirit who lives within me, can You carefully guard the truth I've learned today? Don't let anything steal it away. Help me to not pull back, but move closer to You, where You want me to be. In Jesus' name, amen.

DRAWING FROM THE WELL

- Jeremiah 32:38
- Exodus 25:8
- Genesis 3:8–9
- Revelations 21:3

Paneled Walls

"Is it a time for you yourselves to be living in your paneled houses, while this house remains a ruin? ...You have planted much, but have harvested little... Give careful thought to your ways... Why?" declares the Lord Almighty. "Because of my house, which remains a ruin, while each of you is busy with his own house... the heavens have withheld their dew and the earth its crops."

—Haggai 1:4, 6–7, 9–10

WHEN I READ TODAY'S VERSES, THE FIRST THING THAT comes to mind is my grandparents' house in the 70s with the paneled walls! They were all the rage. All the really far-out houses had them back then. Home renovation shows today are still trying to come up with ways to deal with the paneling. Back in Bible times, paneled walls were a big deal too, but they were made of solid wood. It was something royal families had in their homes. If you've ever watched *Downton Abbey*, you've seen how elaborate royal paneling can be.

These scriptures tell about the time when the Israelites came back to Jerusalem after their captivity. They were so grateful to God for bringing them back to their homeland that they immediately began to rebuild the temple. But then they got sidetracked and started to rebuild their own homes. They stopped working on the temple. God made it clear to them through the prophet Haggai that their inactivity in completing what God had called them to do was the reason they were experiencing lack.

How important it is for us to quickly respond in obedience to what God calls us to do. How frustrated God must get with us when *He* brings us out of something and we let the excitement and thankfulness give way to selfishness. So don't put up any paneled walls in your life. Quickly, move forward in what God has called you to do!

PRAYER:

Father, thank You for Your patience in dealing with me. Please reveal any areas where I have held back in fulfilling Your calling on my life. Help me to build up Your kingdom! In Jesus' name, amen.

DRAWING FROM THE WELL

- Haggai 1:2–9
- Matthew 6:33
- 1 Kings 6:38–7:1
- Luke 12:31, Matthew 6:33

Whose Authority?

Who authorized you to rebuild this temple and restore this structure?

—Ezra 5:3

As soon as the Israelites started rebuilding the temple, the governor of their area halted operations and questioned their authority to do the job. I love the Israelites' answer: "We are the servants of the God of heaven and earth, and we are rebuilding the temple." They went on to explain that they were working under the authority of King Cyrus's decree. They knew who they were and whose authority they were working under!

Too many Christians don't know who they are and the authority that has been given to them. If you don't know those two fundamental truths, you need to familiarize yourself with scriptures that teach on them because the enemy will always use people to make you question if you have any right to do what God's called you to do.

Matthew 28:18 says, *"Jesus came to them and said, 'All authority in heaven and on earth has been given to me.'"* In Luke 10:19, Jesus says, *"I have given you authority..."* Romans 8:11 says, *"And if the Spirit of him who raised Jesus from the dead is living in you..."*

You have been given authority through Christ to accomplish all that He's called you to do. So, when people question you, make sure you know whose authority you're working under!

PRAYER:

Father, I thank You for adopting me into Your family and making me a child of the King! Help me to grow in understanding of my position and authority as Your child. May I walk in the confidence, boldness, and authority of a King's kid! In Jesus' name, amen.

DRAWING FROM THE WELL

- Ezra 5:3
- Matthew 28:18–20
- Luke 10:19–20
- Romans 8:11

The Reset Button

Now then... governor... stay away from there. Do not interfere with the work on this temple of God. Let [them]... rebuild this house of God... The expenses of these men are to be fully paid out of the royal treasury... Whatever is needed... must be given them daily without fail...

—Ezra 6:6–9

A LITTLE WHILE AGO, TODD AND I BOUGHT NEW electronic door locks. We couldn't get the code to work and tried everything in the troubleshooting section of the instructions. There was only one option left, and that was to press the reset button. I held that button down and heard the mechanism reset. I was then able to start over and set the code properly.

God allowed the Israelites to hit the reset button in life. At the end of their seventy-year Babylonian captivity, God called them to rebuild the temple that had been destroyed. God had Cyrus the king of Babylon decree for them to rebuild the temple; the king even committed the government of Babylon to paying for it! Reset button hit.

With excitement, the people laid down the foundation. Then they got sidetracked by their own stuff and set aside the temple building project to build their own homes. Almost twenty years passed and God reminded them of this call to rebuild the temple through the prophets Haggai and Zechariah. The people then repented and began to rebuild the temple with their own money. Reset button hit again.

The local governor saw how they were rebuilding and stopped them. The governor sent a letter telling the new king, Darius, about their work in the hopes of having them blocked from ever rebuilding the temple again. Instead, King Darius sent a letter reinstating King Cyrus's decree. God hit that reset button again and gave them a second chance to do what He had called them to do. This time, they completed it!

A few years ago, I went back to my former Bible college for a reunion. It was great to reconnect with people I hadn't seen for decades. Previously, leadership had moved the school out of the campus where I had attended, and this was the first year they were back in the old facilities. A former classmate, Kevin Johnson, spoke, talking about how he felt God had hit the reset button for the college. He explained how he felt the Lord saying He was also hitting the reset button on the lives of some of the people attending. I knew the Lord was speaking to me.

God has hit the reset button in my life. This time, I will complete my task!

PRAYER:

Father, thank You for second chances. Please forgive me for the decisions I made in the past that veered from your plan. Help me to complete all that You've called me to do! In Jesus' name, amen.

DRAWING FROM THE WELL

- Ezra 6:6–9
- 1 John 1:9
- Jonah 1:1-3, 17
- Jonah 2:1–10

Uncertainty

I therefore so run, not as uncertainly; so fight I, not as one that beateth the air...
—1 Corinthians 9:26, KJV

AT A FAMILY GET-TOGETHER, WE CELEBRATED FIVE KIDS graduating from high school, college, and university. Most of the conversation consisted of answers to the question "What are you going to do...?" Some had clear paths ideally matched to their giftings, while others didn't have a sweet clue what to do and shared their concern over the uncertainty.

Sometimes we feel like we're just shadowboxing, or fighting as one that *"beateth the air,"* seemingly running this race of life aimlessly. It can be frustrating when we're uncertain what the future holds while others around us have such clarity.

The uncertainties of life can be draining, until you recognize that, as Christians, our future is certain. Paul encourages the Ephesian believers that he was praying God would give them the *"Spirit of wisdom and revelation"* so they would know *"the hope"* to which he had called them (Ephesians 1:17–18). Jeremiah 29:11 assures us that God has hope and a good plan for our futures. So if we put these two verses together with our faith, we can know that there truly are no uncertainties. We can let the frustration and stress depart as we relax in knowing that God has it all figured out and we're not aimlessly running the race. Our Father, who is all-knowing, has a good plan for our lives, and He will reveal it to us!

PRAYER:

Father, I thank You for Your plan for my life. I ask that You would continue to bring revelation about the details, as I need to know them. Help me to trust You in this journey of faith. In Jesus' name, amen.

DRAWING FROM THE WELL

- 1 Corinthians 9:26
- Ephesians 1:17–18
- Isaiah 11:2
- Jeremiah 29:11

Hovering

...like an eagle that stirs up its nest and hovers over its young, that spreads its wings to catch them and carries them on its pinions.

—Deuteronomy 32:11

I AM A MOM. I'VE GIVEN BIRTH TO TWO AMAZING PEOPLE (not really kids anymore), but there are many who call me "mom." A bunch affectionately call me their "other mom," and some their "camp mom." Wherever I am, I tend to mother those around me. No matter their age, there's something in me that wants to make sure everyone is okay and to help people reach their God-given potential. I love how today's verse explains that God is a hovering parent too!

As the perfect parent, God can make perfect decisions, knowing when to hover, when to stir up, and when to catch His kids. As my children have gotten older, it's been a real learning process in knowing when to pull back my hovering gift!

Eagles are a perfect example of how to parent people of all ages. When eagles have young, they hover over and provide for every need the eaglet has. When the eaglets get a little older, but before they're ready to leave the nest, before they can fly, the mother, in love, pushes them out of the nest! Now, what kind of parenting is that? Actually, it's great parenting! Great leadership! The eagle then spreads its wings to catch the learner and carries them on their pinions. Understanding that pinions are the wings an eagle uses to fly helps you to understand that they're teaching the eaglet how to fly by example.

Pushing people out of the nest when they're not quite ready accomplishes so many things. It causes the one pushed to place their trust in the one who pushed them, the one who will catch them before they crash. After a few pushes, their confidence grows until one day the eaglet soars!

So, is God pushing you out of the nest or encouraging you to let someone else in your care learn to fly? Take that leap of faith and trust that Your Father is a hovering parent who never lets anyone hit the bottom when you trust in Him!

PRAYER:

Father, I thank You for believing in me! Help me not to fear, but to jump out of the nest and learn to soar. May I fly in Your strength, accomplishing all that You have for me to do. May I push those You have placed in my care to even higher heights than I can go! In Jesus' name, amen.

DRAWING FROM THE WELL

- Deuteronomy 32:11
- Timothy 1:6
- Deuteronomy 33:12
- Philippians 1:6

Catch Me

...like an eagle that stirs up its nest and hovers over its young, that spreads its wings to catch them and carries them on its pinions.

—Deuteronomy 32:11

A FEW YEARS AGO, I TOOK TODD, HIS DAD PHIL, AND MY kids to the drag races. I just couldn't have my hubby not knowing what it's like to have tire rubber all over his face!

We were having a great day, and I was easily passing my passion for the drags on to Todd, when we all got hungry. After visiting the food booth I had worked in as a teen, we began the hike back up the stands. About twenty-five feet up, we turned to take our seats and I heard a loud crack. The floorboards literally gave way under me! I felt myself dropping, but thankfully my elbows were out holding the tray of food and they caught my fall. I landed on the upper and lower seat boards.

Feeling like time stood still, I stared in disbelief, not knowing what to do. The fright in people's eyes made me more fearful. Todd, a few feet ahead but out of reach, quickly stepped on the end of the board, providing a counterweight long enough for Phil to pull me up before the board completely broke.

When I think about this experience and the last part of Deuteronomy 32:11, I'm reminded that no matter how far or how fast I fall, God will catch me!

An eagle spreading its wings to fly under and catch a young eaglet is an incredible visual. All too often, we're like the little eagle, minding our own business when suddenly the floor drops out from under us and we're in freefall.

The crack of the floorboards breaking could be a report from the doctor, a letter in the mail, a call from your bank, or a police officer arriving at your door. Just when you think you're going to hit the ground and be obliterated, God swoops down and catches you, bringing you to safety!

Despite cracking floorboards, freefalls, and times when you question why you're getting pushed out of the nest, understand that God is in fact hovering over you and He will swoop down to catch you when He knows you need a lift!

PRAYER:

Father, I thank You for how You catch me when I'm falling! Help me to trust You when the carpet gets pulled out and I've lost my way. May I rest on Your wings as You fly me safely back to the nest. In Jesus' name, amen.

DRAWING FROM THE WELL

- Deuteronomy 32:11
- Psalm 37:24–25
- Micah 7:7–8
- 1 Corinthians 10:13

God's Incubator

In the beginning God created the heavens and the earth. Now the earth was formless and empty, darkness was over the surface of the deep, and the Spirit of God was hovering over the waters.

—Genesis 1:1-2

...like an eagle that stirs up its nest and hovers over its young...

—Deuteronomy 32:11

WHILE CATCHING UP WITH A FRIEND, SHE TOLD ME THAT she was going through a confusing time and didn't understand what God was up to in her life. She explained this weird, unsettling feeling. I sensed that God was doing something inside her, but she didn't know exactly what was going on. She was in God's incubator!

Today's verse from Genesis came to mind. The word used for God's activity before creating the earth is translated "hovering" in most versions, but the original Hebrew meaning comes from the root word "brood."[8] I learned on my uncle's farm that birds brood by hovering over eggs to keep them hot, like a baby in an incubator. The farmer has to wait until the brooding time is over for the chicks to hatch.

Before God is going to bring something new into the world, or into our lives, the Holy Spirit often hovers and broods over our spirits. During this time, we feel unsettled. Frequently, God moves us into "hot spots" and makes us wait for an undetermined amount of time. The old ways are no longer comfortable; they lack fulfillment. We sense that things are about to change, but we don't know how… or when! It's much like the feeling of a pregnant mother when the baby is getting close to the delivery date.

If you're sensing this in your life, be encouraged; God *is* up to something good. Relax and wait for His perfect timing. Incredible things are birthed in God's incubator!

PRAYER:

Father, I thank You for what You are doing in my life. I may not understand it, but I trust that what You are doing will bring life! Help me to patiently wait while You brood over me. In Jesus' name, amen.

---

8 *Bible Hub*, "7363. Rachaph." Date of access: March 24, 2015 (http://biblehub.com/hebrew/7363.htm).

DRAWING FROM THE WELL

- Genesis 1:1–2
- Deuteronomy 32:11
- Genesis 41:1, 8, 14–16
- Daniel 2:1, 19, 27–28

Desensitized

Having lost all sensitivity, they have given themselves over to sensuality so as to indulge in every kind of impurity, with a continual lust for more.

—Ephesians 4:19

"Did you hear about Jen? Did you hear what John did? Can you believe them? And to think she used to sing in the choir and he used to teach Sunday school!"

It's always shocking when strong Christians fall away from their faith and into sin so scandalous that even unbelievers are appalled. When you read Ephesians 4:19 on its own, you would think it must be about people who didn't know Christ, but it's talking about *Christians* losing the spiritual sensitivity they used to have until they end up totally desensitized.

It's something you think could never happen to you, but I want to warn you that it can happen to anyone who leaves their spiritual thirst unquenched. I feel like God has allowed me to live out an example of this, which seems ironic, being the author of *Water in the Desert*. In one of the sickest weeks of my life, I ended up in the hospital twice for dehydration. A nasty virus left my body depleted, in need of rehydration through an IV. On the first trip to the hospital, I knew I was dehydrated. The second time I was shocked to find out that not only was I dehydrated, but my potassium was also dangerously low. They had to run an EKG to check that my heart hadn't been affected. At one point I almost left the hospital when the doctor was taking too long. I thought to myself, *It's not as bad as last time.* Actually, it was worse.

When people are spiritually thirsty, they notice it. They can sense the Holy Spirit nudging them to go to church, read their Bible, pray, listen to Christian music, call a Christian friend, or to stay away from something. But after a while of being dehydrated, they become desensitized to their spiritual thirst, and that leads to all sorts of ungodly living. The way to stay spiritually sensitive is to stay spiritually hydrated!

PRAYER:

Father, thank You for the water of Your Word! May Your Word hydrate me to overflowing so that I'll stay forever sensitive to Your leading and Your love! In Jesus' name, amen.

DRAWING FROM THE WELL

- Ephesians 4:18–20
- Colossians 3:5
- Psalm 119:11
- Psalm 37:31

Stay in the Water

I commend you for reading this devotional, *Soul H2O*, and drawing from the well of God's Word for yourself. I pray that God refreshed you as you read, making your spirit sensitive to what He is saying to you.

But don't let the flow stop here! Grab a new devotional book and keep in the Word. If you haven't read my book *Water in the Desert*, you might want to check it out. The devotions are a little longer and it has a study guide at the back. My hubby Todd even illustrated it! Just make sure you choose something that helps you stay in the water, like when you were a kid and prolonged your time in the pool so much that your skin wrinkled all up—but you loved it!

Stay spiritually hydrated and let the Living Water quench your spiritual thirst!

Be blessed and refreshed,

About the Author

Sherry Stahl, author of *Water in the Desert*, is a dynamic speaker who travels throughout North America at events for women of all ages. She's a fun, passionate Bible teacher whose desire is to lead others to the life-giving Water in the Word! Her weekly Soul H2O devotions bring refreshment to the soul.

Sherry is the Vice President of Operations for Women In Music & Media (WIMM Canada, www.wimmcanada.ca), an organization created to help connect, refresh, inspire, and equip Christian women across Canada who work in the varying fields of media. She is also the Canadian ambassador for the Christian Women In Media Association (CWIMA, www.cwima.org).

Sherry and her author/illustrator hubby Todd Stahl are co-founders of Take the 40-Day Challenge, a program designed for individuals or churches to go through their devotional books—*Water in the Desert*, *40 Days in the Man cave*, and now *Soul H2O*—to build the habit of personal daily devotions. Subscribers receive forty days of short emails that coincide with the books. Churches can choose programs that include fun weekly videos to inspire their congregation to form fulfilling personal devotional lives.

Growing up in a drag-racing family and her ten years of experience as the part-owner and Director of Finance and Operations for a very successful business in the automotive industry has prepared Sherry to speak comfortably to girls as well as guys. These experiences are an asset to her consulting business as a certified speaker, business coach, and life coach with The John Maxwell Team.

Sherry likes the open road, so when she has free time you can find her cruising in her Mustang with the top down or riding on the back of Todd's Harley!

To learn more about the author, her writings, and speaking engagements, please visit her websites:

www.sherrystahl.com
www.takethe40daychallenge.com

Linked in   Sherry Stahl

twitter   sherry_stahl

Instagram   sherry_stahl

facebook.   Sherry Stahl—Author/Speaker/Blogger

Bringing Water to People in Need

At least ten percent of proceeds from this book will be given to ministries who bring clean water to people in need. Partner with Sherry and these ministries to create a greater impact!

 Water Projects

More than 780 million people do not have access to clean water. Crossroads Relief & Development is helping people access these essential, life-giving resources. Through sustainable initiatives and agricultural programs, Crossroads has helped more than 100,000 people access clean water!

He makes our "deserts like Eden...wastelands like the garden of the Lord." Isaiah 51:3 (NIV)

www.crossroads.ca/relief-development

Know someone else who should *Take The 40 Day Challenge?* Meet the men's counterpart to *Water in the Desert* and *Soul H2O: 40 Days in the Man Cave,* by Todd Stahl!

> "*A man needs another man to talk to him about the deep stuff... Todd Stahl is that man, and 40 Days in the Man Cave is that straight talk. It's clear, fair, honest, and true. Have a listen yourself.*"
>
> —Mark Buchanan
> Author of *Your Church Is Too Safe*

Guys, we all know life is crazy busy. We can be inundated with tasks, jobs, commitments, and activities. The truth is, men need to find a place to get away, chill out, and reenergize. Wherever your man cave may be, carve out

Just 10 Minutes a Day to Change Your Life!
www.takethe40daychallenge.com

What people are saying

Soul H2O is a refreshing cup of fellowship that brings life-sustaining words pouring out like a stream from the heart of Father God himself. This incredible devotional exploding with life giving stories and scriptures will help readers discover the limitless wells of Salvation where the most refreshing of all waters can be drawn. This book is a powerful, poignant reminder that God is the source of joy, refreshment and strength in times of need.

—Rachelle Fletcher
Dallas, TX
Singer, Songwriter, Speaker,
Senior Director of Development
Human Coalition DFW
www.rachellefletcher.com

Like a tall glass of water on a sizzling hot day, Sherry's insightful devotions help us drink deeply from the truth of God's faithfulness to us, no matter what the circumstance. Using real life examples paired with Scripture, she will help you start each day with hope and purpose.

—Cheryl Weber
Burlington, ON
Co-host *100 Huntley Street*
International Producer
Crossroads Relief & Development
www.crossroads.ca

God used Sherry's words to speak directly to me, in ways she'll never know. The devotionals are quick but profound, and minister to that thirsty spot in our hearts that God so wants to water!

—Sheila Wray Gregoire
Belleville, ON
Award-winning author of
The Good Girls Guide To Great Sex
Speaker and Blogger
www.tolovehonorandvacuum.com

With incredible insight and wisdom, Sherry inspires you with *Soul H2O*. Whatever you may be facing in your life, Sherry will help you draw from the refreshing well of God's word."

—Sue Detweiler
Frisco, TX
Author of *9 Traits of A Life-Giving Mom*
Radio Host and Pastor
www.suedetweiler.com

Sherry's authentically loving personality is evident in these quick but compelling devotions. Each is a reminder of how our relationship with God has a powerful impact in the midst of our busy lives.

—Ruth Thorogood
North York, ON
Executive Director, The Word Guild
www.thewordguild.com

I believe we all have a thirst in our soul that can only be quenched by living water. Come and drink from the well-spring of God's Word, and allow His Spirit to refresh your life! Sherry Stahl shares from her own heart and pours into yours in an honest, relatable and practical way. Soul H2O provides not only wisdom and inspiration, but also an encouraging reminder that you are not alone. Enjoy with delight!

—Karol Ladd
Dallas, TX
Author of *The Power of a Positive Woman*
Speaker and Blogger
www.positivelifeprinciples.com

Reading *Soul H2o* is like sitting on a cozy couch, with a warm blanket, a hot cup of tea and Sherry right beside you, encouraging you in your relationship with Jesus. This devotional is written from authentic life experience and filled with the powerful Word of God. If you're thirsty for hope, encouragement and direction then this should be on your bedside table!

—Sarah E Ball
Lethbridge, AB
Author of Fearless in 21 Days, Blogger
www.saraheball.com

Sherry's refreshing devotional thoughts draw from a deep well of experience & the even deeper well of Living Water through God's Word. They're perfect for those wanting a short daily dose of encouragement, as well as those wanting to dig in further to the Word for themselves! Enjoy!

—Ellen Graf-Martin
Elmira, ON
President of Graf-Martin Communications
Speaker and Communicator of Hope
www.ellengrafmartin.com

Uplifting, inspiring, and encouraging, *Soul H2o* offers us sweet sips of truth that both satisfy and convict us to believe God at His Word. I changed while reading this book. Sherry's words challenged me to embrace God's purpose for me, and to trust that my Savior will always carry me through the most difficult trials and transform them into blessing. *Soul H2o* is an essential devotional for a thirsty soul that longs to be quenched.

—Jennifer Strickland
Southlake, TX
U R More Founder and Speaker
author of *21 Myths (Even Good) Girls Believe About Sex*
www.urmore.org

Affirmation from Regular Soul H2o Blog Readers

I have grown tremendously over the last few years reading Sherry's *Soul H2O* devotions. The blogs are life giving and relate to the needs of Christians today. I am encouraged, strengthened and renewed weekly; reminded that God's sovereignty prevails and because of Him, I have power to overcome any obstacle.

—Erica Heil
Ruthven, ON
Bible Study Leader,
Secondary School Teacher, GECDSB
Special Education, Family Studies

Have you ever felt like you were drowning with no life raft in sight? Thankfully, God is always there but sometimes He seems VERY distant. Sherry has a unique and powerful way of reminding us that God is our Father and VERY involved in our lives. Each week I look forward to seeing her e-mails and blogs appear with the needed "fresh drink"!

—Georgia Martin
Calgary, AB
Interior Designer
Owner, Creative Touch by Georgia
www.creativetouchbygeorgia.com